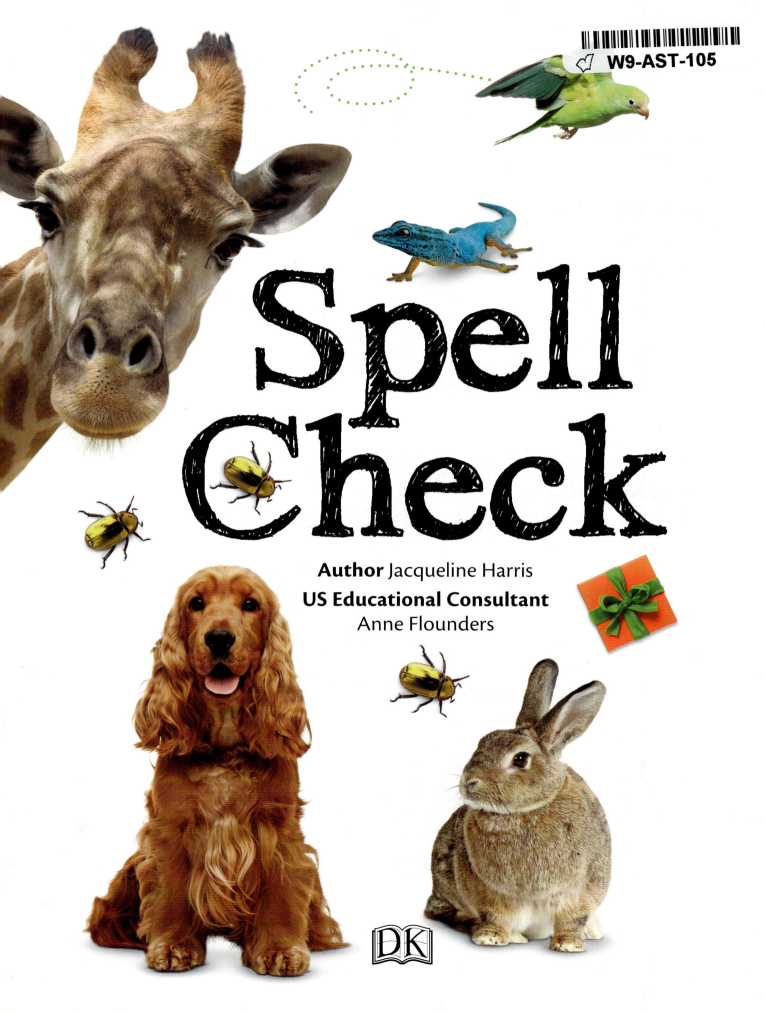

Spell Check

Author Jacqueline Harris

US Educational Consultant
Anne Flounders

DK

Contents

Tips   Rules   Activities

Spell Check

pair

pear

All the spelling rules and more than 2,000 words!

leaf

T i ger

Butterfly

leaves

Butterf l i es

Important note to you!

The more you learn about spelling, the more enjoyable and useful you'll find it.

Why learn to spell?

Spelling is an incredibly useful tool. Correct spelling allows other people to read and understand what you have written. Learning about spelling also gives you a bigger vocabulary to use in your writing and make it more interesting and powerful.

Can't I rely on a dictionary or spell checker?

There are lots of reasons why learning to spell correctly is much better than relying on a book or a machine. Here are three of them:

1. If you have no idea how to spell a word, you will not be able to look it up in a dictionary, nor will the spell checker recognize which word you want.

2. Spell checkers also do not recognize mistakes with homophones (words that sound the same but are spelled differently) or typing mistakes like this regular one: "form" instead of "from."

3. Most importantly, neither a dictionary nor a machine will be able to tell you that there is a much better and more exciting word you could be using instead.

Why do I need this book?

This book will give you the RULES for many common spellings, show you how the rules work, and provide examples. When you learn the spelling rules, you find the meanings of so many new words, and you have words that can bring your writing to life. While there are a great many rules, there are also words that follow no rule at all and just have to be learned. This book will point out these EXCEPTIONS.

How it works:
nut + **s** = nut**s**
Examples:
squirrel → squirrel**s**
tree → tree**s**
stick → stick**s**
tail → tail**s**

Then you can practice the rules and test yourself with finding new words and links in spelling patterns on the ACTIVITY pages.

look cover write check

This book will also give you TIPS on how to learn spelling, because not everyone likes to learn in the same way. By the end, you will have found a few different ways that help YOU remember spellings, as well as a regular practice section called "look, cover, write, check."

Look out for the animals, because they're eager to help you and give examples about how the spelling rules work!

Meet the phonics word families

I am Marlee, a proud mother hen! Just look at my fluffy family of four chicks. Aren't they sweet? They are a bit noisy, though! We are the **/ee/** sound family, but my chicks have names that have the sound spelled differently than mine. There's Peach, Eve, Bobby, and Finley.

Phonics

A word for how sounds (phonemes) and letters (spelling patterns) make words. English has 44 different phonemes, and most of these have several different ways (at least) of spelling them.

Use what you know about **phonics** as your first step when trying to spell an unfamiliar word. Then see if the word looks right and, if not, try a different spelling pattern for a sound.

Good idea!

Long vowel sounds

/ai/ (tr**ai**n), **/ee/** (f**ee**t), **/igh/** (n**igh**t), **/oa/** (b**oa**t), **/oo/** (f**oo**d), **/u-e/** (t**u**b**e**)

Short vowel sounds

/a/ (h**a**t), **/e/** (p**e**t), **/i/** (s**i**t), **/o/** (d**o**t), **/u/** (h**u**t)

Digraphs and trigraphs

When you have two letters together that make just one sound, it is called a **digraph** (for example, **sh** in "ship"). When you have three letters together making one sound, it is called a **trigraph** (for example **igh** in "high").

CAN YOU use your phonics knowledge to sound out and spell the names of these animals?

Start thinking!

What is the plural of squirrel?

tails

I am a very hungry squirrel. A hungry squirrel needs lots of nuts to eat. Nuts is the plural of nut. Plural means "more than one." Without plurals, I could only have one nut. Did I mention that I was hungry?

legs

Just add an "s"

This, in a nutshell, is the first rule of making plurals. To form the plural of most nouns, add **s**.

nut

nuts

How it works:

nut + **s** = nut**s**

Examples:

squirrel → squirrel**s**

tree → tree**s**

stick → stick**s**

tail → tail**s**

ears

lakes

foxes

boxes

sandwiches

lunches

watches

beaches

buses

glasses

cows

classes

dishes

schools

dresses

princes

toes

knees

princesses

RULE

Add "es"

Many words are made plural with the addition of an **es**. This sounds like **/ez/**. To form the plural of nouns ending in **s**, **x**, **z**, or **ch**, just add **es**.

How it works:

bench + **es** = bench**es**

Examples:

grass → grass**es**

buzz → buzz**es**

class → class**es**

pass → pass**es**

grass

grasses

Owls or owles?

Whoooooo wants to practice more plurals? Come on, it'll be a hoot. Remember, if you add an **s** to a word and it sounds like **/ez/**, it is spelled **es**. Listen for the extra sound at the end.

Fill-in fun

Complete the lists with either "s" or "es" to make plurals.

1 goat, 3 ...goats.........   1 girl, 3 ....

1 team, 3 ....   1 weed, 3 ....

1 toy, 3 ....   1 patch, 3 ....   1 night, 3 ....

1 kiss, 3 ....   1 bench, 3 ....   1 wish, 3 ....

The big finish!

Try turning these nouns into plurals.

witch ....

wand ....

cat ....

spell ....

wizard ....

Super-silly sentences

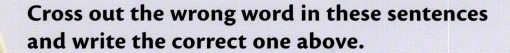

Cross out the wrong word in these sentences and write the correct one above.

The owls sit on the branchs.

I saw some foxs in the woods.

The magic potiones turned the tables into chocolate.

The witch lit the candles with some matchs.

We learned lots of spelles in our lessons.

We waved our magic wandes and the owl disappeared!

Double up

Rewrite this magic spell, but make all the singular words plural.

Note: You may need to change or cut out some other words, too.

The witch added an eye of a frog, a feather of a bird, a tail of a horse, and a scale of a fish.

....

....

....

Sing a spelling

I am a noisy songbird. I know a trick that may help you learn your spellings: turn the rule or a particular spelling into a rhyme or mini song.

Music is a useful way to learn, and a rhyme or tune can help you remember. Sing a song with me!

Good idea!

p e o p l e

To the tune of Happy Birthday to You:

"p-e-o-p-l-e, p-e-o-p-l-e, p-e-o-p-l-e, that's how you spell people."

plural rule

To the tune of Humpty Dumpty:
"For most plurals, just add an **s**,
that just means there is more than one,
but some plurals sound like **/ez/**
then you know you add **es**."

CAN YOU?

CAN YOU pick a rhyme you know well?

Make up a rhyme for spelling this word.

surprise

Start thinking!

Turn this rule into a different rhyme.

plural rule

Why, wolf, y?

I am a curious wolf cub, and I enjoy exploring with the other babies. It's more fun when there is more than one! That's when the lone wolf becomes a pack of wolves. Howl!

RULE

"y" to "i" then add "es"

If a word ends in **y**, the plural changes the **y** to an **i** before adding **es**. BUT for words ending in **ey**, **ay**, or **oy**, just add an **s**.

strawberry

strawberries

How it works:

baby − **y** → **i** + **es** = bab**ies**

Examples:

lady → lad**ies**

city → cit**ies**

strawberry → strawberr**ies**

look cover write check

RULE

"f" to "v"

If a word ends in **f**, the plural changes the **f** to a **v** before adding **es**.

Watch out for any noun that has the **/f/** sound at the end of it—even if it is spelled **fe**, like in "life." The plural also ends with **ves.**

How it works:

wolf – **f** ➜ **v** + **es** = wol**ves**

Examples:

calf ➜ cal**ves**

knife ➜ kni**ves**

life ➜ li**ves**

wife ➜ wi**ves**

calves

calf

centuries

ladies

families

skies

bodies

teddies

memories

halves

hooves

selves

wives

loaves

scarves

knives

lives

keys

journeys

monkeys

Two's company

Give these animals some company by making the plurals.

dog ....

bee ....

duck ....

fox ....

Word swap

Rewrite these phrases, turning the words in bold into plurals.

Note: You may need to change or cut out some other words, too.

A **wolf** in the dark **wood** ....

A **baby** in the **crib** ....

A **lady** with a **loaf** of bread ....

A **horseshoe** on the **hoof** ....

Which one doesn't belong?

Which of the words in each line doesn't belong when they are made plural? Circle the word.

dog   pig   (fish)

Fish is the one that doesn't belong, because you add **es**, not just **s**, to make the plural.

calf   cow   bull

bear   canary   butterfly

puppy   fly   porcupine

 # Time for a tune

Turn the rule about changing "y" to an "i" and adding "es" into a song.

You can either use one of the tunes you used on page 11 or try a new tune, such as "Mary Had a Little Lamb."

I'm not a regular sheep

I am a sheep and I don't follow the rules. On my own, I'm just me: a sheep. But when a flock of us get together, we are not sheeps, we are still sheep. It's not baa-d spelling, it's just that "sheep" is an irregular plural. Remember: If you can't sleep, don't count sheeps; count sheep.

sheep

Baaa!

hooves

hoof

RULE

Stay the same

Some words, like "sheep," stay the same as singular and plural.

Examples:

sheep

moose

deer

fish

pants

All change

Other words completely change when they become plural.

Examples:

mouse ➜ mice
goose ➜ geese
man ➜ men
tooth ➜ teeth
child ➜ children

geese

woman

women

child

children

salmon

scissors

louse

lice

person

people

foot

feet

bison

moose

cactus

cacti

jeans

tights

A herd of rhinos or rhinoes?

I belong to a herd of rhinos. We are one of a group of animals that have a vowel ending that's not an **e**. This means that we have our own rules for plurals. Don't get this wrong or we'll get angry and we'll charge!

RULE

Add "s" or "es"

If a word ends in **a**, **i**, or **u** just add an **s**. If a word ends in **o**, add an **es**. BUT this is not true for words like rhino, hippo, dodo, disco, and photo.

banana

bananas

Watch out! There are some exceptions with words like "antenna," which become "antennae."

Examples:

volcano ➔ volcano**es**

tomato ➔ tomato**es**

gnu ➔ gnu**s**

cobra ➔ cobra**s**

banana ➔ banana**s**

gorilla ➔ gorilla**s**

photo ➔ photo**s**

Note

My longer name is "rhinoceros" but in a herd, we can become a group of "rhinoceroses." What a mouthful! No wonder our name is often shortened.

How it works:

rhino — rhino**ceros** →
rhino**ceros** or
rhino**ceroses**

Examples:

photo — photo**graph** →
photo**graphs**
hippo — hippo**potamus** →
hippo**potami** or
hippo**potamuses**

look
cover
write
check

banana

potato

potatoes

flamingo

flamingoes

photos

rhinos

volcanoes

tomatoes

buffaloes

taxis

zebras

sofas

llamas

kiwis

orchestras

dramas

gorillas

Sort it out

Write these animals in their plural form in the correct column:

monkey, moose, butterfly, mouse, fish, penguin, wallaby, fox, armadillo, snake, eagle, pony

Just add "s"

....
....
....
....
....
....

Add "es"

....
....
....
....
....
....

Change to "ies"

....
....
....
....
....

Irregular

....
....
....
....
....

Animals' alphabet

Think of an animal for every letter of the alphabet and write the plural name on each line.

Check your spellings in a dictionary.

A ....

B ....

C ....

D ....

E ....

F ....

G ....

H ....

I ....

J ....

K ....

L ....

M ....

N ....

O ....

P ....

Q ....

R ....

S ....

T ....

U ....

V ....

W ....

X ....

Y ....

Z ....

Does it look right?

Spelling can be a very prickly job! The spelling of some words follows the rules, but for other words you just have to learn how to spell them. To help you learn, just try to spell the word and see if it looks right.

And for an extra prickly tip: If it looks wrong then try again, maybe by using a different way of spelling the same sound.

Good idea!

p o r c u p i n e

por is spelled just like it sounds, and **pine** follows the rules. But the middle part sounds like **/q/—porqpine**. This doesn't look right! There would never be a **q** next to a **p**. So either look the word up in a dictionary or try again.

Follow these steps:

Step 1

What sounds can you hear when you say the word? How many sounds can you hear? Are there any sounds that have two letters or more?

Step 2

Try to spell the word yourself and then see if it looks right.

Step 3

If it doesn't look right, then try again, then check with an adult or in a dictionary.

CAN YOU try spelling the names of these animals, using the three steps?

Start thinking!

Hopping around letters

I am a grasshopper and I have a challenge for you! I just can't keep still, and neither can the letters in my name. The letters want to hop around and make new words of all different lengths.

How many different words can you make with the letters in "grasshopper"?

Good idea!

Start by thinking of the different digraphs you can use—for example **er**, **sh**, and **oe**. Can you find any others? Put them as headings in the boxes. Then see how many different words you can make using the letters.

s h

shape

rash

e r

o e

g r a s s h o p p e r

Good idea!

It might help to cut the letters out on a piece of paper and move them around, or use a piece of paper to try out spellings and see if they look right.

Cats vs dogs

I am a cat who does regular catlike things.
I can walk and jump, and curl up to sleep.
These action words are verbs that tell
you what I'm actually doing.

Add "ed" or "ing"

For regular verbs, just add **ed** at
the end for the past tense, meaning
it has already happened; and just
add **ing** for the present tense,
which means it is happening now.

HOW it works:

walk + **ed** = walk**ed**

walk + **ing** = walk**ing**

Examples:

jump → jump**ed**, jump**ing**

crawl → crawl**ed**, crawl**ing**

I am a dog who does regular doglike things, which are slightly different than cats. I can hug and rub, and drip from my mouth.

RULE

Double up

For regular verbs with a short vowel sound in them double the end consonant when in the past or present tense.

HOW it works:
hug + **ed** = hug**ged**
hug + **ing** = hug**ging**

Examples:
rub → rub**bed**, rub**bing**
drip → drip**ped**, drip**ping**

The exception to the doubling rule is for words that end with **x**. Never double **x**! mix → mix**ed**, mix**ing**

guard

guarding

guarded

appear

appeared

appearing

protect

protected

suggest

suggested

trip

tripped

skip

skipping

strapped

fix

fixed

fixing

What makes pets amazing?

We are amazing pets. We can dance and dazzle, bounce and dive, explore and race. And what's more amazing is that all our verbs end with an **e**!

Verbs ending with "e"

When a verb ends with **e**, take the **e** off and then add **ing** for the present tense, OR just add the **d** for the past tense.

racing

How it works:

dance – **e** + **ing** = danc**ing**

dance + **d** = dance**d**

Examples:

explore → explor**ing**, explore**d**

dazzle → dazzl**ing**, dazzle**d**

love → lov**ing**, love**d**

dive → div**ing**, dive**d**

dazzling

Note

Some strange verbs don't follow this rule. Some verbs ending in **e** are irregular and completely change (see pages 32–33), and other verbs like "agree" become agree**d** or agree**ing**.

look
cover
write
check

refuse

slide

breathe

exercise

notice

promise

surprise

suppose

type

continue

believe

complete

decide

describe

increase

guide

scare

save

Right or wrong?

Cross out the regular verbs that are spelled wrong.

jumped   danceing   growlling   bounced

fixxed   dived   joging   mixing

raced   explord

Double or not

Sort these verbs into the two columns.
Write them in the past tense.

notice, hop, groan, like, slip, plan, share, enjoy, ask, use, stop

Double the consonant for the past tense	Do not double the consonant for the past tense
....	....
....	....
....	....
....	....
....	....
....	....
....	....

Which one doesn't belong?

Which of the words doesn't belong when they are in the past or present tense? Circle the word.

walk   jump   (hop)

Hop is the word that doesn't belong, because it is the verb that doubles the consonant in the past and present tense.

like	hug	hope
bake	pull	help
count	skip	grab
play	paint	run

Time challenge

How many verbs can you think of in four minutes? Then turn the words you have written into the past tense.

(If you have written irregular verbs—see pages 32–33—they don't follow the rules and completely change in the past tense.) Remember: To spell the verbs, sound them out and use phonics to help you.

....

....

....

....

....

....

....

What makes a platypus irregular?

I am a duck-billed platypus and quite unusual. I'm a furry mammal, but I have a duck's beak and lay eggs. You could say that I'm completely irregular and certainly don't follow the rules for being a mammal.

Irregular verbs

Irregular verbs don't follow the rules when they change to the past tense. The only way to learn them is to remember them. Say a sentence out loud and listen to hear whether it sounds right.

Examples:

drink ➜ drank

say ➜ said

make ➜ made

come ➜ came

throw ➜ threw

eat

ate

are

were

see

saw

shake

shook

meet

met

catch

caught

bite

bit

sell

sold

speak

spoke

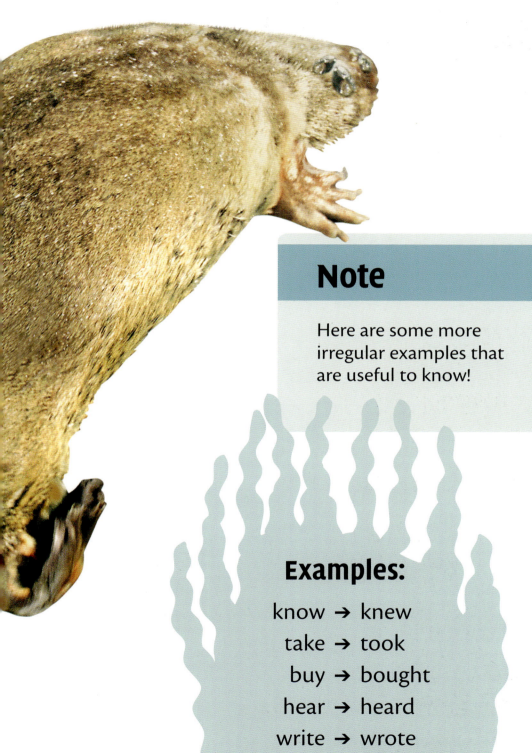

Note

Here are some more irregular examples that are useful to know!

Examples:

know ➔ knew

take ➔ took

buy ➔ bought

hear ➔ heard

write ➔ wrote

feed ➔ fed

sleep ➔ slept

How to compare elephants

biggest

I am the smallest elephant in the herd. I like to compare myself with my dad, who is bigger and heavier than me. At the water hole, I can be the wettest and the muddiest, though. Watch out! I'll squirt you!

big

RULE

"er" and "est"

Sound the trumpet! Here are the important rules. When comparing two things, add **er** to the word. When something is the topmost thing, then add **est** to the word.

How it works:

tall → tall**er** → tall**est**

Examples:

small → small**er** → small**est**

slow → slow**er** → slow**est**

weak → weak**er** → weak**est**

fast → fast**er** → fast**est**

Add "r" or "st"

For words already ending in **e**, just add **r** or **st**.

For words with a short vowel sound, double the end consonant before adding the ending.

For words ending in a **y**, change to an **i** before adding the ending.

bigger

Examples:

large → larger → largest
big → bigger → biggest
wet → wetter → wettest
heavy → heavier → heaviest
happy → happier → happiest

large

larger

largest

older

oldest

longer

longest

broader

broadest

tiny

tinier

tiniest

lazy

lazier

laziest

deeper

deepest

straight

straighter

heavy

heaviest

Who is the biggest?

Squeak! I'm surrounded by animals bigger than me, but I'm quicker than most. The tiger looks the scariest to me!

You choose!

Which word is the best fit? Cross out the other word.

The hippo is **(larger/largest)** than the zebra.

The antelope can run **(faster/fastest)** than the bison.

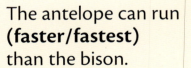

The little monkey can climb into the **(higher/highest)** branches of the trees.

The water buffalo is the **(muddier/muddiest)** of all the animals at the water hole.

The tiger is the **(fiercer/fiercest)** of all the big cats.

Compare challenge

Write the correct label for the animals.

smallest   tallest   youngest

heaviest

Fill-in fun

Complete the lists by writing the words with
the suffixes "er" and "est."

happy _happier, happiest_ ....   scary ....

loud ....   large ....

quiet ....   noisy ....

What makes playful cubs fearless?

We are playful bear cubs, full of happiness and enjoyment as we search for honey. You can have fun, too, describing how things are happening by adding the suffixes **ment**, **ful**, **less**, and **ness** to words. Don't be fearful; be fearless like us!

Suffixes and root words

Adding suffixes does not usually change the spelling of the root word.

How it works:
care + **ful** → care**ful**

Examples:
sad → sad**ness**

hope → hope**less**,

hope**ful**

enjoy → enjoy**ment**

Change "y" to "i"

For words ending in **y**, which have more than one syllable, change the **y** to an **i**.

How it works:

happy – **y** → **i** + **ness** → happ**iness**

Examples:

merry → merr**iment**

creepy → creep**iness**

joy → joy**ful**

amuse → amuse**ment**

pain → pain**less**

bright

brightness

lonely

loneliness

achieve

achievement

develop

development

fear

fearful

fearless

cheer

cheerful

graceful

restless

breath

breathless

purposeful

What's the ending?

Choose a suffix

Choose the suffixes "ment," "ful," "less," or "ness" to add to each of these words to describe these lion cubs.

rest ....

beauty ....

enjoy ....

color ....

naughty ....

Sentence challenge

Write a sentence using each of the following words.

purposeful ....

....

....

excitement ....

....

....

harmless ....

....

....

Find the meaning

"ful" means "full of"
"less" means "without"
"ment" means "as a result of an action"
"ness" means "a state of"
Use these meanings to make one word.

without care <u>careless</u> ....

without harm ....

the state of being kind ....

full of cheer ....

move as a result of an action ....

Missing word

Use the words you made in the activity above.
Put the correct word into these sentences.

They showed great .... when they looked
after the bird.

She knew the snake was ...., because she had read
about it in a book.

Having the dog made the old man feel very ....

The cat watched the .... of the bird and got
ready to pounce.

John made a big mess when painting the house because
he was ....

Who nests here?

I'm a cuckoo and I'm too lazy to make my own nest, so I lay my eggs in other birds' nests. I like the robin's nest, the warbler's nest, and the magpie's nest. The apostrophe shows who the home belongs to and to how many.

cuckoo's wing

RULE

Apostrophe

When something belongs to one thing or person, the possessive apostrophe (') is used, followed by an **s**.

How it works:

burrow of the rabbit →
the rabbit**'s** burrow

Examples:

the cat**'s** basket
the bear**'s** den
the fox**'s** den

the cat's basket

cuckoo's tail

Plural apostrophe

RULE

When something belongs to more than one thing or person, just the apostrophe is added after the plural.

Except for irregular plurals, when the apostrophe is still before the **s**.

How it works:

hive of the bees ➔ the bee**s'** hive

nest of the mice ➔ the mice**'s** nest

Examples:

the pig**s'** sty

the parrot**s'** perch

the children**'s** game

stopped

really

because

better

clothes

morning

window

friends

animals

would

again

after

everyone

wanted

something

mother

place

cried

Whose home?

Match the animals to their homes and write in the list underneath.

kennel   hive   hole

coop   aquarium   dovecote

stable   lodge   barn

the dog's kennel ....

....

....

....

....

Right the wrong

Put the apostrophe in the correct place in these sentences.

The girl got the horses saddle from the rack.

The mices nest was snug and dry.

The pigs supper was some acorns, which it ate very quickly.

It is Ibrahims birthday today.

I went to the childrens playground with my friends.

The leopards fur is covered with a spotted pattern.

Time challenge

How quickly can you use an apostrophe to transform these phrases?

The horse belonging to the girl ...the girl's horse...

The cats belonging to the ladies ....

The sty belonging to the pig ....

The fur belonging to the bear ....

The hooves belonging to the buffaloes ....

The lair belonging to the wolf ....

How to spell the /igh/ in fly

I am a tiny fly, but I can fly really high just like a spy plane with my amazing eye. Oh my! Is that a mighty-sized pie I spy?

The /igh/ sound

There are several different ways you can spell the **/igh/** sound. With so many choices, try to spell a word and see if it looks right.

pie

How it works:

igh → h**igh**

split digraph **i-e** → l**i**k**e**

ie → p**ie**

eye → **eye**

capital letter **I**

ei → h**ei**ght

y → sp**y**

Note

/**igh**/ is the most common sound the letter **y** makes at the end of words. But the letter **y** can also make the /**ee**/ sound at the end of words, as in "happy."

Examples:
fly, try,
my, reply,
why, sky

replied

deny

decide

polite

prize

cried

surprise

guide

height

buy

by

bye

fried

pie

nice

comply

eye

slight

Fill-in fun

Read the clues and then complete the missing letters in these words.

Most birds can do this.

f_y

Make something bigger with a special piece of glass.

magn_fy

Follow instructions.

c_mply

Tell someone you did not do something.

de_y

Use the missing letters to make the name of a fierce animal.

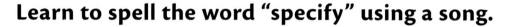

Time for a tune

Learn to spell the word "specify" using a song.

You can either use one of the tunes you used on page 11 or try one of your favorite tunes.

You choose!

Choose the right word to complete these sentences. Cross out the other word.

The tiger cubs (**rely/reply**) on their mother.

The students (**supply/apply**) for the job.

The witnesses (**guide/identify**) the thief.

The desert was (**defy/dry**).

Word sort

Does the letter "y" make the sound /ee/ or /igh/? Sort these words into the two columns.

happy, fry, ordinary, apply, supply, century, probably, why, imply, July, lazy, actually, rely

/igh/ sound	/ee/ sound
....	....
....	....
....	....
....	....
....	....
....	....
....	....
....	....

Why are gorillas great?

I may look like a gentle giant, but I'm actually a great gorilla. It's all in the **g**'s. "Gentle" and "giant" have a soft **g** like a **/j/** sound, while "great" and "gorilla" each have a hard **/g/** sound. Grrr.

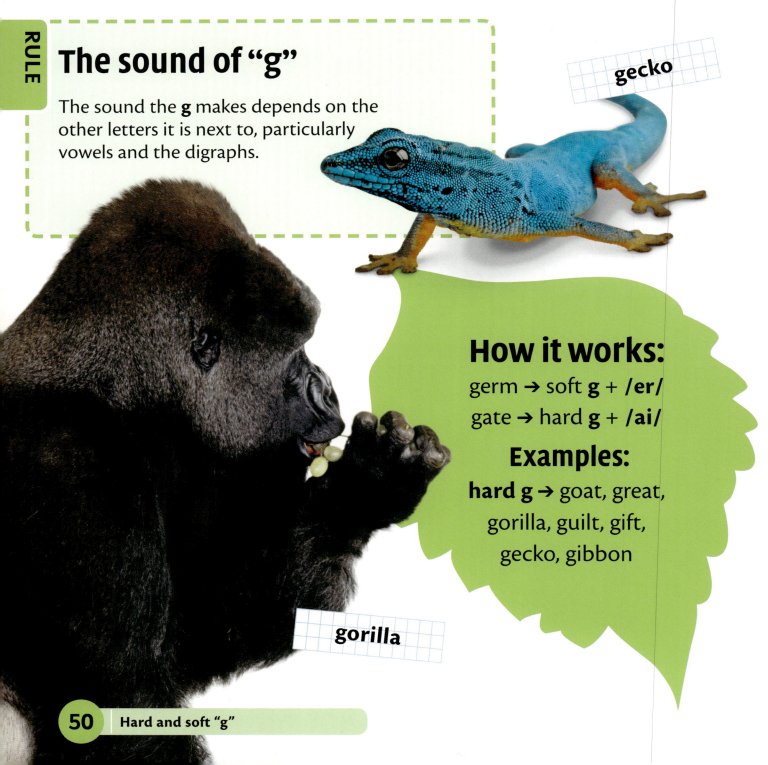

gecko

The sound of "g"

The sound the **g** makes depends on the other letters it is next to, particularly vowels and the digraphs.

How it works:

germ → soft **g** + /er/

gate → hard **g** + /ai/

Examples:

hard g → goat, great, gorilla, guilt, gift, gecko, gibbon

gorilla

gerbil

Examples:

soft g → gerbil, giraffe, giant, ginger, gym

giraffe

group

grammar

guard

great

giraffe

gentle

fudge

bridge

dodge

magic

danger

energy

germ

gentleman

Egypt

gym

gymnastics

gorilla

Why are giraffes and goats different?

Are you ready to solve this mystery? Complete the following detective work and then write your own clues so that you will remember this spelling.

Clue 1

Sort these words into two lists: soft "g" or hard "g."

goat, giant, get, gum, giraffe, game, glad, gear, general, gem, germ, ginger, good, grape

Soft "g"	Hard "g"
....	....
....	....
....	....
....	....
....	....
....	....
....	....
....	....
....	....
....	....

Clue 2

Add some of your own words to each list in Clue 1.

Clue 3

Write some more words of your own that have the "g" somewhere other than the beginning; for example, "dodge" or "fling."

....

....

....

....

Conclusion

Look at the detective's final report. Search for and underline the soft "g" and circle the hard "g" wherever they appear.

When I went to the zoo, I saw a huge range of animals. There were large

giraffes and a great gecko. The goats tried to get my gloves! Looking

suspicious was the giant panda, but I also suspected the grizzly bear,

which greeted me with a grin as I gazed through the glass.

Life at the North Pole

I am a polar bear, and I'm equipped and prepared for the extreme cold here at the North Pole. I've been watching the scientists working here though. They have to deice their vehicles before they can set out and there can be no mistakes, because it is dangerous to be out in the cold unprepared.

Prefixes "un," "dis," or "mis"

When the prefix **un**, **dis**, or **mis** is added onto a word (the root), it does not change the spelling of the word, but only the meaning. The word turns into the opposite or negative of the original root word.

How it works:

un + prepared → **un**prepared

mis + lead → **mis**lead

dis + like → **dis**like

Examples:

appear → **dis**appear

fortunate → **un**fortunate

understood → **mis**understood

Note

Not all words have a root word that still makes sense on its own. You can make a "mistake," but not a "take."

disappear

disapprove

disabled

disagree

discount

disconnect

misspell

mislay

misfit

misfortune

misunderstand

misuse

uncomfortable

uncommon

unable

uneasy

undo

uneven

Fill-in fun

Add the correct prefixes "un," "dis," or "mis" to the incomplete words in the following paragraph.

The scientists came to study

the polar bear, whose habitat is slowly

........appearing. They were ....happy

about what they ....covered. While they

were ....certain of the exact problem, it was

clear that there was no ....take; the polar bears

were becoming rarer.

What's the opposite?

Use "un," "dis," or "mis" to make these words mean the opposite.

dress ....dress

comfort ....comfort

behave ....behave

understand ....understand

connect ....connect

All change!

Rewrite each of these sentences, changing its meaning.

I like fruit. I dislike fruit.

My brother agreed with me.

....

The rider mounted the horse.

....

Write one sentence of your own using a "mis," "dis," or "un" word used in "What's the opposite?"

....

....

....

....

Word bank

Here are some great words you could use in your writing. Find the definition of each of them and then impress your teacher by using them in your writing.

disgruntled ....

misfortune ....

unkempt ....

An elephant never forgets

They say an elephant never forgets anything. **"Mnemonics"** is a very tricky word for a way of remembering some of the more complicated spellings.

Good idea!

A **mnemonic** is any device or strategy that helps you remember something.

because

big **e**lephants **c**an't **a**lways **u**se **s**mall **e**xits

rhythm

rhythm **h**as **y**our **t**wo **h**ips **m**oving

necessary

it is ne<u>c</u><u>ess</u>ary to have one
<u>c</u>ollar but two <u>s</u>leeves

CAN YOU?

**CAN YOU create a mnemonic for each
of these words?**
Will you still remember them in a few days' time?

guard

answer

occasion

How do desert snakes survive?

SSSs. It is exxxxceptionally hot here in the dessssert. I am a rattlesssssnake and I ssssleepily ssssstay coiled under a rock until ssssslithering ssssswiftly out to hunt once the sssssun hassss gone down.

Suffix "ly"

The suffix **ly** turns an adjective into an adverb, so the word describes the action rather than the object. For most adjectives, just add **ly** to turn it into an adverb.

How it works:

slow + **ly** → slow**ly**

Examples:

quiet + **ly** → quiet**ly**

unfortunate + **ly** → unfortunate**ly**

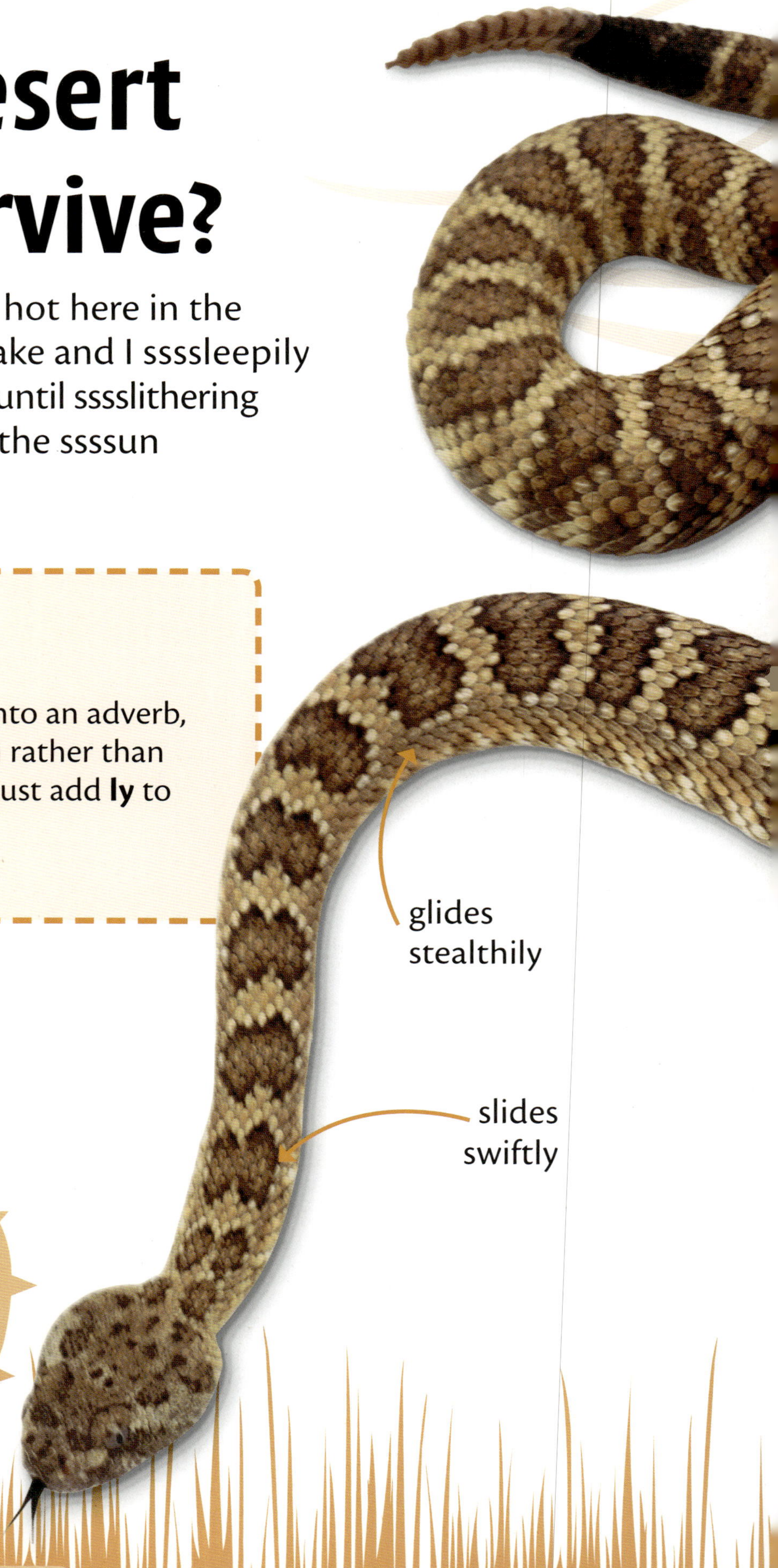

glides stealthily

slides swiftly

Adding "ly"

RULE

For words ending in **y**, the **y** changes to **i** before adding the **ly**.

For words that end in **le**, drop the **le** to add **ly**.

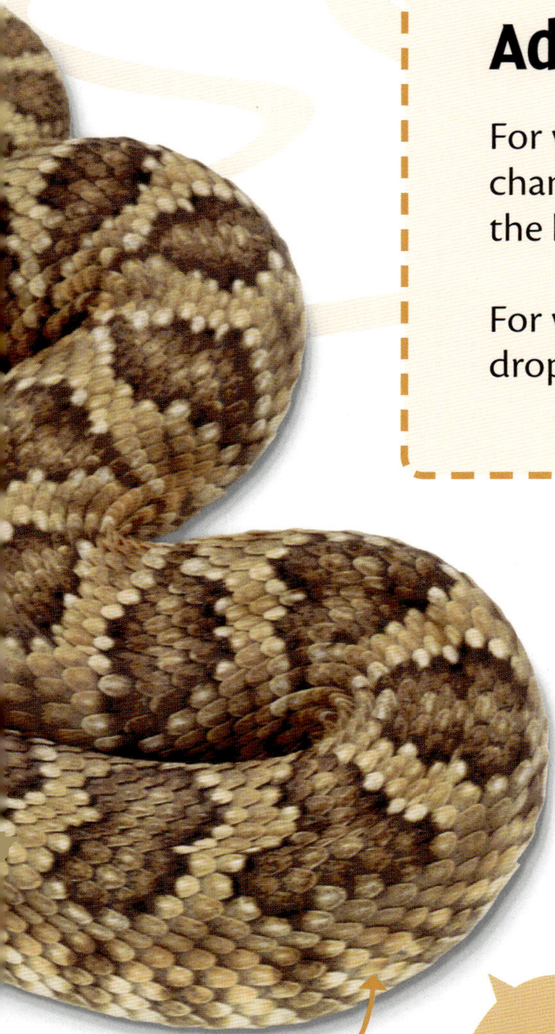

uncoils gracefully

How it works:

angry – **y** → **i** + **ly** → angr**ily**

possible – **le** + **ly** → possib**ly**

Examples:

happy → happ**ily**

easy → eas**ily**

comfortable → comfortab**ly**

horrible → horrib**ly**

look cover write check

properly

furiously

splendidly

carefully

smoothly

bravely

possibly

comfortably

easily

horribly

lightly

friendly

regularly

seriously

probably

accidentally

occasionally

recently

How do insects behave?

Buzz! The bees are buzzing angrily. The ants are marching briskly. How are the other insects in the garden behaving?

Lively labeling

Complete the labels on the picture to describe how you think the creatures are acting, using adverbs with "ly."

butterflies fluttering
....

bees buzzing
....

beetles scuttling
....

Missing word

Add the adverbs to these sentences, picking the correct one from the list below.

quietly	possibly	accidentally
lightly	bravely	

Bob spoke ....

The butterfly landed .... on the flower petal.

The man .... knocked the glass over, and it broke into a thousand pieces.

Harry .... attacked the wasp before it stung the baby.

Tomorrow I may .... be going to the park, but I am not sure.

All change!

Change these adjectives into adverbs.

happy ..happily..................   peculiar ....

naughty ....   regular ....

special ....   careful ....

strange ....   easy ....

surprising ....   sudden ....

What's your position, pigeon?

I am a pigeon, but you won't find me in a park or a station because I'm a clever racing pigeon. Whatever my location, I can find my way back home. So to avoid confusion, look out for my identification tag.

The /shun/ sound

The **/shun/** sound is mostly (but not always) spelled **sion** after the **/l/**, **/r/**, **/s/**, and **/n/** sounds. Otherwise the **/shun/** sound is spelled **tion**.

action

motion

How it works:
confuse → confus**ion**
subtract → subtract**ion**

Examples:
discuss → discuss**ion**
invent → invent**ion**

station

information

position

mention

imagination

fiction

addition

subtraction

multiplication

division

confusion

expression

invention

discussion

reception

description

creation

education

Fact or fiction?

Fiction quiz

**Look at the list of stories that all feature animals.
Then answer the questions.**

Three Billy Goats Gruff	Goldilocks and the Three Bears
Three Little Pigs	Alice in Wonderland	Henny Penny

Who went into the bears' house without permission?

....

Who had a very strong imagination so was not
surprised to see a white rabbit with a watch?

....

What animals are tempting the hungry troll whose
position is under a bridge?

....

Who created confusion by thinking that
the sky had fallen in?

....

What was the wolf's mission when he blew
down the houses?

....

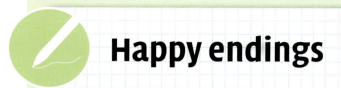

Happy endings

tion *sion* *tion* *sion*

Add the correct suffix to these words, using "tion," or "sion."

prevent ..prevention.................................

create ....

discuss ....

describe ....

imagine ....

express ....

authorize ....

revise ....

Word bank

Here are some interesting words. Find the definition of each of them and then use each word in a sentence.

confusion ....
....

information ....
....

invention ....
....

subtraction ....
....

education ....
....

How are you today, gray horse?

I am a very special horse because I pull the Queen's carriage in parades for important occasions. There are eight horses like me and we have very fine reins. At the start of her reign, the Queen was drawn in a carriage pulled by white horses, but we are beige or gray.

The /ai/ sound

There are several different ways you can spell the **/ai/** sound. With so many choices, try to spell a word and see if it looks right.

eight

How it works:

ai → tr**ai**n

ay → pl**ay**

the split digraph **a-e** → m**a**k**e**

ei → **ei**ght

ey → th**ey**

a → **a**corn

ea → br**ea**k

Note

The digraphs **ai** or **ei** are rarely at the end of a word, but **ay** or **ey** are used at the end of a word.

ay is sometimes found in the middle of a word, too, like in "crayon."

they

gray

say

rein

beige

apron

sleigh

weight

eight

made

scrape

veil

dismay

paint

remain

translate

obey

escape

Missing words

Fill in the missing words to complete the description of the horses.

gray	eight	they	sleigh
reins	neighing	mane	stable

These are fine .... colored horses, each with long

.... for the riders to hold. In winter, when it is snowy,

they sometimes pull a .... They make a loud noise

called .... stay in a

.... at night and there are .... stalls

altogether. Each one has a beautifully cared-for ....

Sound families

Begin a list of the words with different spellings of the /ai/ sound.

ai	ay	a
rain	stay	agent
....	....	....
....	....	....

ei	a-e	ey
beige	snake	they
....	....	....
....	....	....

Add the labels

Label each of the pictures. Each word has the /ai/ sound, but which spelling does it use?

....

....

....

....

....

....

....

Is that a fowl or foul on the field?

I am a fowl, but don't confuse me with a foul between players on a soccer field. Otherwise you will be saying, there was a duck on the field! Don't confuse me for a foul rainy day either, or else you'll be saying it's pouring with ducks!

RULE

Homophones

Homophones are words that sound the same but are spelled differently and have different meanings. The only way you can know these spellings is to learn them and learn their meanings.

How it works:
fowl / foul

Examples:
rein / reign

right / write

Note

It is important to know the right homophone, because a computer spell-checker would not be able to figure out if this was not the right word.

tail (not tale)

feet (not feat)

to

too

two

there

their

they're

bear

bare

write

right

by

buy

eight

ate

here

hear

peace

piece

Dear Deer

to? *too?* *to?* *two?*

Help Deer by filling in the correct "to," "too," or "two" in the gaps in her letter!

too?

two?

to?

Dear Deer,

How are you? I have been meaning .... write .... you for .... weeks now, but I have been .... busy at school. We have been learning all about homophones. How are things in the forest? If you'd like .... catch up, meet me at .... o'clock. Bring your friends the squirrels, ...

Hello!

From me!

You choose!

Choose the right homophone to complete these sentences.

The boat sailed in (**fare/fair**) weather.

Dad (**mist/missed**) the train to work.

The boy ties a (**not/knot**) with his shoelaces.

The tired storekeeper took a (**break/brake**).

The lion had a majestic (**main/mane**).

Match up!

Match the words below to the correct picture.

knight

flower

hair

hare

bear

night

flour

Silly sentences

Correct the mixed-up homophones in these silly sentences.

I couldn't wait to meat my friends. ....

Because I overslept, I mist the bus. ....

I had a long weight for the next bus. ....

The mouse got his tale caught. ....

I'm an international sea turtle

I am a sea turtle. Welcome to my watery world. I may seem antisocial, but I'm an international traveler and I migrate hundreds of miles. I automatically follow the currents from the USA to Indonesia and back again. Oh no! I can see a plastic bag littering the seabed and damaging the environment. If only that bag had been recycled!

Prefixes and root words

Each of the prefixes **anti**, **auto**, **inter**, **re**, and **sub** comes from Latin. They each have a meaning that changes the meaning of the root word they are attached to.

How it works:

anti = against or opposite →

antisocial = not wanting the company of others

Examples:

auto = the same or self → **auto**biography = a book about yourself

inter = between → **inter**national = involving different countries

re = again → **re**arrange = arrange it again differently

sub = beneath or below → **sub**marine = below the water

redo

refresh

return

reappear

redecorate

antidote

antisocial

autograph

automobile

automatic

subheading

submerge

submarine

interactive

interest

internal

interrupt

international

Note

Sometimes, root words are not words on their own. For example, with the word "interrupt," there is no such words as "rupt"!

Examples:

react

antiseptic

automatic

internet

subway

Prefixes | 77

Match up!

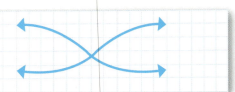

Match the prefixes to the ends of words to make complete words.

Prefix	End of words	Completed words
anti	rupt	....
auto	merge	....
inter	biotic	....
re	turn	....
sub	matic	....

You choose!

Choose the correct word in each of these sentences. Cross out the other word.

I am going to (**reinvent/recycle**) these bottles.

When Suzy kept talking, the teacher asked her to please not (**interrupt/interval**) in the middle of the lesson.

In the intermission of a show, you can buy (**reforms/refreshments**).

The famous film star was asked for his (**autobiography/autograph**).

The crocodile was completely (**substantial/submerged**) under the water.

Which one?

Choose a prefix that can be added to the words in each row to make new words. Write the complete words.

Prefixes:	re	sub	anti	auto	inter

cepted	act	lock	....
tract	marine	ject	....
cracy	pilot	mobile	....
affirm	cord	heat	....
social	climax	dote	....

Word bank

Choose four words with its prefix from the list above.

For each word, find out what it means and write it in a sentence.

....

....

....

....

....

....

....

How to remember the echidna

I am an echidna. I'm a very unusual type of creature that lives in Australia. You may never have heard of me before, and my name is certainly a very tricky word to spell. So here are some ideas that might help you remember my name.

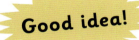

Good idea!

Have a picture in your head of the word as well as the animal so that it sticks in your brain and looks familiar.

Write the word ten times.

echidna

echidna, echidna, echidna, echidna, echidna, echidna, echidna, echidna, echidna, echidna

Think! This animal looks a bit like a hedgehog.

Split up the word into pieces.

e-chid-na

Use phonics, although this word does not sound the same as it is spelled.

Turn the word into a picture.

echidna

It has tall letters in the middle and shorter ones either side.
Notice the word **hid** in the middle.

CAN YOU follow these three steps with these words?

country

gardening

Watch out for the rat!

I am the rat in separate. Separate is one of the most commonly misspelled words. Even adults do not always know how to spell it!

To remember that it's an **/ar/** sound, not an **/er/** sound, in the middle of sep**arat**e, remember **a rat**!

Good idea!

Sound out the word.

s – e – p – ar – a-e – t

There's a split digraph near the end of this word.

Find the word within.

s e p - a-rat- e

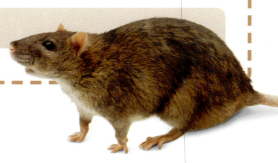

Write the word ten times.

separate

separate, separate, separate, separate, separate,

separate, separate, separate, separate, separate

CAN YOU sound these words out and find the hidden word?

peculiar

business

disappoint

Let's talk!

"Who's a pretty bird?"
That's me! I'm a talkative parrot. I don't use formal words. I've learned to talk using **contractions**. They're very useful for chatty birds like me.

RULE

Contractions

A contraction is when two words (or more) are joined together and parts of the word are left out. The missing part is replaced with an apostrophe.

How it works:

I + **a**m → I'm

Examples:

do n**o**t → don't
they **are** → they're
would n**o**t → wouldn't
can **no**t → can't
we **wi**ll → we'll

Note

Using contractions is a very casual way of writing, and if it is a piece of writing, such as a formal letter or a piece of information, there should not be any contractions in the work.

didn't

couldn't

you'd

what's

I'm

let's

they're

won't

should've

o'clock

we're

how'd

doesn't

haven't

I'll

isn't

aren't

it'll

Cat rescue

Change the contractions to full words to correct this class's newspaper report about a cat that was stuck in a tree.

Yesterday at our school **we'd** .... seen a cat.

Our teacher said we **shouldn't** .... scare the cat, but one

boy **didn't** .... listen and the cat ran up a tree. Our teacher said

we **shouldn't** .... climb the tree to rescue the cat because we

won't .... be able to get down. But Freya said **she's** ....

a good climber and **she'd** .... be able to get the cat.

She's .... a very good climber and she did climb the tree.

I thought the cat might get frightened, but **it'd** .... sat

watching us all and **wasn't** .... at all scared. Clever Freya

managed to get the cat down safely and our teacher said **she'd**

.... been very brave.

One-minute challenge

Can you turn the following words into a contraction within a minute?

he is ....   that will ....

do not ....   could not ....

Sentence challenge

Write a sentence for each of the following contractions.

there's ....

....

isn't ....

....

o'clock ....

....

shouldn't ....

....

where'll ....

....

You choose!

Some contractions are also homophones that are often used incorrectly. Choose the right spelling in each sentence. Cross out the wrong words.

I've got (**your/you're**) book by mistake.

(**They're/There/Their**) going to the farm by bus.

(**Whose/Who's**) coat is that?

(**Its/It's**) a really sunny day today.

Word art

I am a dolphin and I love to **leap** and **twirl**. My name is tricky to spell as it has a **ph** and not an **f** in it.

Turn the word you are learning to spell into a picture to help you remember it.

Good idea!

dolphin

tremor

CAN YOU turn these words into a picture?

bounce

rainbow

CAN YOU?

Is it a cat or a civet?

I am a civet. Don't confuse me with a cat! I'm a completely different animal. My body is a different shape than a cat. My name begins with a different sound, too. Although civet is spelled with a **c**, the sound it makes is **/s/**.

The letter "c"

The letter **c** makes the widest range of sounds in the English language.

/k/ → **c**at
/s/ → **c**ivet
/q/ → **c**ue
/sh/ → spe**c**ial
/x/ → a**cc**ess

Sound change

The letters or letter strings following the **c** changes the sound the **c** makes.

How it works:

c + **a**, or **o** = /k/ → **ca**t or **co**t

Examples:

c + **e**, **i**, or **y** = /s/ → **ce**iling, **ci**vet, **cy**cle

c + **ia**, **ea**, or **io** = /sh/ → spe**cia**l, o**cea**n, suspi**ciou**s, magi**cia**n

c + **c** = /x/ → a**cc**ept

c + **ue** = /q/ → **cue**

cycle

look cover write check

calendar

special

center

century

certain

caught

circle

complete

continue

decide

describe

experience

increase

sentence

actually

bicycle

exercise

difficult

Word sort

carrot cardigan accident magician

Sort these words into the sound the "c" makes.

carrot, cardigan, accident, magician, column, disco, cylinder, cue, access, celebrity, ocean, mercy, octopus, Canada, cereal, except, December, celery

c = /k/	c = /s/	c = /sh/	c = /q/	c = /x/
....	....	....	....	....
....	....	....	....	....
....	....	....	....	....
....	....	....	....	....
....	....	....	....	....
....	....	....	....	....
....	....	....	....	....
....	....	....	....	....
....	....	....	....	....

Add some of your own words to each list.

Word art

Choose a word from each list and create a word picture.

Can you include in each picture what sound the "**c**" makes to help you remember the rules?

Ssh for the little lamb

In the springtime, I leap and run around the field. I'm just a little lamb, so then I need to take a rest. Quiet, please! You can't hear all the letters in my name. The **b** is silent. You'd never know it was there.

Silent letters

The only way to spell words with silent letters correctly is to find a way of remembering that silent letter. Start by actually sounding out the letter.

gnome

How it works:

friend ➔ **i** is silent ➔ say fr**i**-end

Examples:

knight ➔ **k** is silent ➔ say **k**-night

gnome ➔ **g** is silent ➔ say **g**-nome

i**s**land ➔ **s** is silent ➔ say i**s**-land

choc**o**late ➔ the second **o** is silent

➔ say choc-**o**-late

thumb

scissors

friend

knight

lamb

column

Autumn

island

difference

definite

dictionary

January

February

medicine

knife

jewelry

vegetable

family

Note

Look out for unstressed or silent letters in all sorts of words.

chocolate

Quiz master

All the answers to these questions have a word with a silent letter.

Make sure you do not leave the letter out when you write the answer!
Note: Check the spelling of your answers with a dictionary or an adult.

What is a baby cow called?

....

Which is the second month of the year?

....

Which subject at school includes the study of maps?

....

A carrot is a type of what?

....

Which two things can you use for cutting something?

....

What is a piece of land entirely surrounded by water?

....

Which delicious sweet brown food melts when it gets too hot?

....

Letter hunt

Use a colored pencil to highlight the unstressed or silent letters in each word.

wrinkle

guide

gnash

sandwich

wrapping

disguise

interest

kneel

foreign

climb

science

castle

listen

biscuit

Word bank

Here are some words with silent letters. Find the definition of each of them and then use each word in a sentence.

wreckage ....

....

chaos ....

....

doubt ....

....

What are your thoughts?

I am a Shire horse. Look how big and tall I am. I need to duck to avoid the boughs. As I worked through the day, I thought about returning to my stable at night for my food and water in the trough. I would eat and drink until I'd had enough.

Letter strings

ough is a very common spelling pattern. Although the same four letters are together, they make a different sound, depending on the word.

trough

How it works:

/ow/ → b**ough**

/off/ → tr**ough**

/oo/ → thr**ough**

/u/ → bor**ough**

/o/ → th**ough**

/uff/ → en**ough**

/aw/ → th**ough**t

More strings

igh, **ear**, and **ie** are other common spelling patterns that make several sounds. Watch out for these in words!

How it works:

/igh/ → h**igh**

/ai/ → we**igh**t

/ear/ → h**ear**

/air/ → p**ear**

/ur/ → **ear**n

/igh/ → p**ie**

/ee/ → ni**e**ce

pie

pear

height

weight

pear

earn

field

niece

thieves

tried

cough

enough

thought

through

though

thorough

tough

rough

dough

trough

Word sort

although *trough* *enough* *thought*

Put the words in the correct column for the sound of the letter string "ough."

ought, bought, rough, cough, borough, dough, although, trough, thorough, enough, tough, thought, through

/off/	/uff/	/o/	/aw/	/oo/
....	....	....	....	....
....	....	....	....	....
....	....	....	....	....
....	....	....	....	....
....	....	....	....	....

Memory mnemonics

Write mnemonics for two of the words above.

....

....

....

....

....

....

....

....

Picture this

Create a word art using one of the words on page 100.

Rhyme time

Write a rhyming word for each of these words.

Note: The spelling of the rhyming words does not have to be the same because it is only the sound that matters.

pear ..hair............................

weight ....

learn ....

sigh ....

through ....

bough ....

tough ....

fear ....

cough ....

which sow?

I am a sow and the proud mother to my many little piglets. See how they are very happily playing next to me in our sty. Nearby, the farmer is plowing the field, ready to sow some seeds. I hope the noise won't upset my piglets.

Homographs

Homographs are words that are spelled the same, but have different meanings. Sometimes they are even pronounced differently.

bow

How it works:

sow = to plant seeds

sow = female pig

Examples:

bow = bend over to show thanks

bow = a knot for tying shoelaces or decorative ribbon

look
cover
write
check

Note

Sometimes homographs are pronounced the same but still mean different things.

change

How it works:

change = to do something differently

change = money given if you have overpaid

Examples:

wave = move of a hand to say hello or goodbye

wave = arch of water sweeping onto a beach

wind

bow

read

saw

tear

can

change

match

park

rock

sink

fine

minute

row

wave

wound

bass

down

Silly sentences

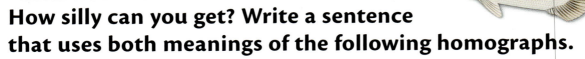

How silly can you get? Write a sentence that uses both meanings of the following homographs.

For example: The **bass** sang in a deep **bass** voice.

tear ....

sink ....

rock ....

wound ....

minute ....

Picture puzzler

Choose two of these homographs and draw a picture for both meanings.

park	match	row	ring	court

Match the meaning

Match the homograph underlined in the sentence to its correct definition.

Check (✔) the correct definition.

Sentence	Definitions	Check
I got a **fine** when my library book was late back.	Everything is ok	
	A charge made for overdue items or illegally parked cars	
When he went under a low branch he had to **duck**.	A water bird, often seen on ponds	
	A verb meaning to move your head down quickly	
The **wind** was blowing wildly through the trees.	A strong gust of air	
	A verb meaning to roll up or turn the movements on a clock	
A **saw** was used to cut the logs smaller.	The past tense of the verb to see	
	A sharp, serrated edged cutting tool	
When I returned home from school, I wanted to **watch** my favorite TV program.	A small clock worn on the wrist	
	A verb meaning to look at	

When does two become one?

We may be tiny creatures, but we all have something in common. No, it's not that we all have six legs and wings—there's something else as well. The clues are in our names: butterfly, honeybee, horsefly, dragonfly, and ladybug. Each of our names is a **compound word**.

butterfly

Compound words

A compound word is when two words are put together to make a new word. The spelling of both the original words stays the same. When a word is added to another, the new compound word has a different meaning.

ladybugs

How it works:

dragon + fly ➔ dragonfly

Examples:

ear + wig ➔ earwig

silk + worm ➔ silkworm

earth + worm ➔ earthworm

Buzz! I'm back to my beehive!

honeybee

earwig

earthworm

housefly

thumbnail

bluebell

birthday

everyone

somewhere

anybody

playground

football

downstairs

goalkeeper

weekend

breakfast

sideboard

backbone

sunshine

Note

Some insects see with compound eyes. Compound means "when things are put together," and many insects have amazing eyes made up of hundreds of cells.

dragonfly

Mixed-up pictures

Join any two words from the list below to make nine new types of insects. Then draw some of them.

fly	body	foot	fast	bell	saw	water	earth
lady	ball	bed	worm	bug	glow	bee	see
	flower	break	dragon	blue	fall	no	

.... foot + fly → footfly............

....

....

....

....

....

....

....

....

Match up!

Create 12 compound words by joining a word from each list.

List 1			
goal	sun	blue	half
birth	every	paint	break
up	any	back	fair

List 2			
stairs	bell	one	keeper
day	fast	body	brush
bone	shine	time	ground

....

....

....

....

....

....

....

Out and about

**Look for some compound words around you and compile
a list of the ones you have seen.**

For example: Place names are sometimes compound words, and there may
be some in the books you are reading.

....

....

....

....

....

Do beetles scuttle or scuttal?

We are busy beetles. We scuttle everywhere on our six little legs. Watch out! We may tickle if we crawl across your hand.

RULE

"le" or "al"

The **le** is the most frequent spelling for this sound at the end of words. If in doubt always choose **le**, rather than **al**.

eagle

How it works:

crump + **le** → crump**le**

Examples:

examp + **le** → examp**le**

tab + **le** → tab**le**

eag + **le** → eag**le**

When to double

If the word has a short vowel sound followed by one consonant, the consonant is usually doubled before adding **le**. (Don't forget: some consonants are never doubled such as **j** or **h**.)

If the word has a short vowel sound followed by two consonants, just add **le**.

If the word has a long vowel sound, or digraph, followed by one consonant, just add **le**.

look cover write check

example

little

people

table

middle

needle

uncle

simple

bicycle

eagle

startle

circle

possible

probable

material

natural

occasional

special

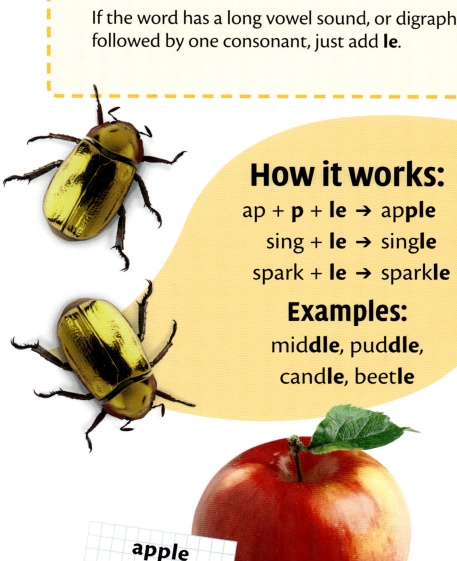

How it works:

ap + **p** + **le** → ap**ple**

sing + **le** → sing**le**

spark + **le** → spark**le**

Examples:

mid**dle**, pud**dle**, can**dle**, beet**le**

apple

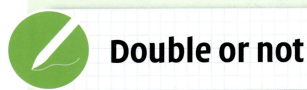

Double or not

Write the answers to these clues. All the answers end in "le."

Remember: Only some consonants are doubled
before adding **le**. (The first letter has been provided.)

The name of this type of insect.

b ....

An octopus has eight of these.

t ....

A hedgehog has lots of these.

p ....

The name of this sea creature.

t ....

A penguin walks like this.

w ....

Time for a tune

**Look back at the two rules about words ending in "le"
on pages 110 and 111 and turn them into a tune to
help you remember them.**

You can either use one of the tunes you used on page 11,
or try one of your favorite tunes.

Word collection

Add more words under each column for each of these word endings.

-ckle	-able
crackle	table

-ible	-dle
horrible	candle

I'm an expressive chimp

Can you guess how I'm feeling? I can make this face. . . and this face. . . and this face. Do you think I look happy or sad? I could be overjoyed or gloomy, glad or miserable. There are so many words to describe how you think I may be feeling, so choose carefully.

Synonyms

Synonyms are words that all mean the same thing. When writing, choose the right synonym to tell someone exactly what things are like.

How it works:

happy → glad, ecstatic, overjoyed

Examples:

sad → glum, miserable, heartbroken

ask → request, demand, interrogate

Antonyms

Antonyms are words that mean the opposite. These words help to show someone how things are compared.

How it works:

speedy / plodding

Examples:

gigantic / microscopic

scorching / freezing

said

told

asked

shouted

yelled

screamed

cried

whispered

muttered

responded

answered

uttered

argued

chattered

stammered

stuttered

babbled

jabbered

Size matters

How "big" is this big whale? How "small" is this small clown fish? Create a list of words that mean big and another list for words that mean small.

Words that mean small	Words that mean big
....	....
....	....
....	....
....	....

Circle the word that best describes the whale and the clown fish.

Showing off!

Suggest five words that mean the same as "beautiful" to describe this peacock.

....

....

....

....

....

Best word

Here is a list of synonyms for "red." Which word do you think best describes these "red" animals? You can use a word more than once.

ruby	scarlet	russet	flushed
flaming	crimson	rosy	

....

....

....

....

....

....

....

In the beginning...

I might be an extinct dinosaur, but I can tell you a thing or two about **root words**. The word "dinosaur" literally means "fearfully great lizard" and many dinosaurs like me have the Greek root word "saur" in their names. I'm stegosaurus, which means "roof or covered lizard." Talking about roots is making me feel hungry. I'll get back to munching some plant roots.

RULE

Root words

A root word is the main part of the word to which other parts have been added. Families of words can all be made with the same root word.

How it works:

camara + **saurus** = chambered lizard

Examples:

ankylo**saurus** = stiff lizard

tyranno**saurus** = tyrant lizard

baro**saurus** = heavy lizard

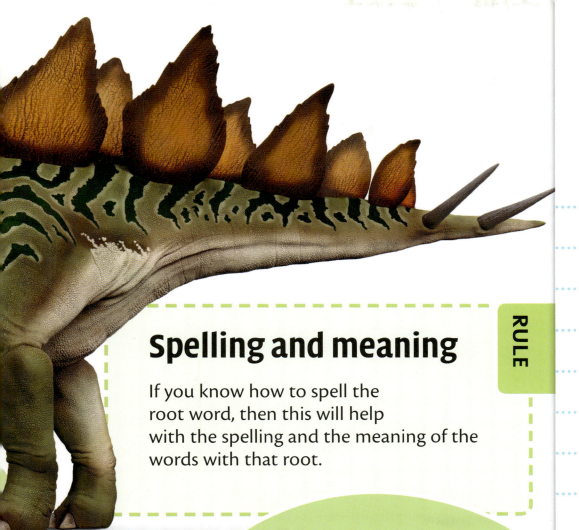

Spelling and meaning

If you know how to spell the root word, then this will help with the spelling and the meaning of the words with that root.

How it works:

sign → **sign**ature, **sign**age, **sign**ify
live → a**live**, surv**ive**, **live**lihood, re**live**

Examples:

phone = sound
→ tele**phone** = sound that travels far
→ **phone**me = smallest unit of sound
→ head**phone**s, ear**phone**s, homo**phone**, micro**phone**

sign

signature

live

change

changeable

answer

answerable

early

earliest

extreme

extremely

heart

perhaps

popular

popularity

remember

remembrance

woman

Do- you-think-it-saurus?

Make a collection of dinosaurs with the root word "saurus" and find out their meanings.

Dinosaur name	Meaning
....	....
....	....
....	....
....	....
....	....
....	....

Word bank

What other words with these root words can you think of?

"graph" (Greek = writing)	"hood" (Old English = person, condition, or quality)	"trans" (Latin = across)
tele**graph**	child**hood**	**trans**late
....	....	....
....	....	....
....	....	....
....	....	....
....	....	....

Root challenge

Determine the meaning of the original root word (shown in *italic*) in these words. Then add two examples of words with each of these "roots."

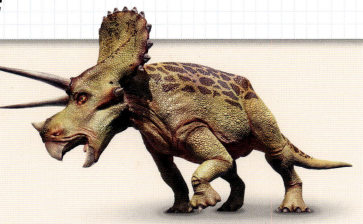

uni as in universe ....

....

bi as in bicycle ....

....

tri as in triceratops ....

....

quad as in quadrilateral ....

....

octo as in octopus ....

....

cent as in century ....

....

mille as in millipede ....

....

Glossary

Adjective
a word that describes a noun; e.g., an *enormous* lion

Adverb
a word that describes a verb, adjective, or adverb, and tells when, where, or how something happened, often ending in **ly**; e.g., John *happily* walked along the road

Antonym
a word that has an opposite meaning to another; e.g., *big* and *small*

Compound word
a word formed when two words are joined together; e.g., *football*

Consonant
the letters of the alphabet that are not vowels

Contraction
shortened form of words, with an apostrophe denoting the missing letter or letters; e.g., should not becomes *shouldn't*

Digraph
two letters that combine to make one sound; e.g., *ph*, *ey*

Homograph
a word that is spelled the same as another word, but has a different meaning and often sounds different; e.g., *park*, *bow*

Homophone
a word that sounds the same as another word, but is spelled differently and has a different meaning; e.g., *dear* and *deer*

Letter string
a spelling pattern with more than one letter; e.g., *ough*, *igh*

Noun
a word that is either an object, a person, or an idea; e.g., *chair*, *cat*, and *grace* are all nouns

Phoneme
the smallest unit of sound a letter or letters make; e.g., *c-a-t* are the phonemes in *cat*

Plural
when there is more than one noun; e.g., three *horses*

Prefix
a letter or group of letters that, when added to the beginning of another word, changes the meaning; e.g., **mis** makes spell *misspell*

Root word
the main part of a word to which other parts are added; e.g., *tricycle*, *triceps*

Singular
when there is one of something; e.g., a *cat* or a *mouse*

Suffix
a letter or group of letters that, when added at the end of another word, changes the meaning and sometimes the spelling of the original word; e.g., happy becomes *happier*

Synonym
a word that has a very similar meaning to another word; e.g., *big, large*

Verb
a word that describes an action; e.g., *run, jump, think, try*

Verb tense
the verb changes according to when it has happened; e.g., in the present—he *is shouting*; in the past—he *shouted*; and in the future—he *will shout*

Vowel
the five letters of the alphabet *a, e, i, o, u*

Answers

Fill-in fun
teams, toys, kisses, girls, weeds, patches, benches, nights, wishes

The big finish!
witches, wands, cats, spells, wizards

Super-silly sentences
branches, foxes, potions, matches, spells, wands

Double up
The witches added eyes of frogs, feathers of birds, tails of horses, and scales of fishes.

Two's company
dogs, ducks, bees, foxes

Word swap
The **wolves** in the dark **woods**
The **babies** in the **cribs**
The **ladies** with **loaves** of bread
The **horseshoes** on the **hooves**

Which one doesn't belong?
calf, bear, porcupine

Sort it out

Just add "s"	Add "es"	Change to "ies"	Irregular
snakes monkeys armadillos eagles penguins	foxes fishes	butterflies wallabies ponies	mice moose

---

Right or wrong?
danceing, growlling, fixxed, joging, explord

Double or not

Double the consonant for past tense	Do not double the consonant for past tense
hopped, stopped, slipped, planned	noticed, groaned, used, liked, shared, enjoyed, asked

Which one doesn't belong?
hug, bake, count, run

You choose!
The hippo is **larger** than the zebra.
The little monkey can climb into the **highest** branches of the trees.
The antelope can run **faster** than the bison.
The water buffalo is the **muddiest** of all the animals at the water hole.
The tiger is the **fiercest** of all the big cats.

Compare challenge
lion cub – youngest
giraffe – tallest
hippo – heaviest
rabbit – smallest

Fill-in fun
loud, louder, loudest
quiet, quieter, quietest
scary, scarier, scariest
large, larger, largest
noisy, noisier, noisiest

40–41

Choose a suffix
restful, beautiful, enjoyment, colorless or colorful, naughtiness

Find the meaning
harmless, kindness, cheerful, movement

Missing word
kindness, harmless, cheerful, movement, careless

44–45

Whose home?
the chickens' coop, the horses' stable, the bees' hive, the fishes' aquarium, the beaver's lodge, the mole's hole, the doves' dovecote, the cow's barn

Right the wrong
The girl got the **horse's** saddle from the rack.
The **mice's** nest was snug and dry.
The **pig's** supper was some acorns, which it ate very quickly.
It is **Ibrahim's** birthday today.
I went to the **children's** playground with my friends.
The **leopard's** fur is covered with a spotted pattern.

Time challenge
the ladies' cats
the pig's sty
the bear's fur
the buffaloes' hooves
the wolf's lair

48–49

Fill-in fun
fly, magnify, comply, deny; lion

You choose!
The tiger cubs **rely** on their mother.
The students **apply** for the job.
The witnesses **identify** the thief.
The desert was **dry**.

Word sort

/igh/ sound:	/ee/ sound:
fry	happy
apply	ordinary
supply	century
why	probably
imply	lazy
July	actually
rely	

52–53

Clue 1

Soft "g"	Hard "g"
giant, giraffe, general, gem, germ, ginger	goat, get, gum, game, glad, gear, good, grape

Conclusion
When I went to the zoo, I saw a <u>huge range</u> of animals. There were <u>large giraffes</u> and a (great gecko). The (goats) tried to (get) my (gloves)! Looking suspicious was the <u>giant</u> panda but I also suspected the (grizzly) bear, which (greeted) me with a sort of smile as I (gazed) through the (glass).

56–57

Fill-in fun
disappearing, unhappy, discovered, uncertain, mistake

What's the opposite?
undress, discomfort, misbehave, misunderstand, disconnect

All change!
My brother disagreed with me.
The rider dismounted the horse.

62–63

Missing word
quietly, lightly, accidentally, bravely, possibly

All change!
naughtily, specially, strangely, surprisingly, peculiarly, regularly, carefully, easily, suddenly

Fiction quiz
Goldilocks
Alice
Goats
Henny Penny
Eat the pigs

Happy endings
discussion, imagination,
authorization, creation,
description, expression, revision

Missing words
These are fine **gray** colored horses, each with long **reins** for the riders to
hold. In winter, when it is snowy, they sometimes pull a **sleigh**. They make
a loud noise called **neighing**. **They** stay in a **stable** at night and there are
eight stalls altogether. Each one has a beautifully cared-for **mane**.

Add the labels
crayons, tray, weigh, reindeer, plane, acorn, train

Dear Deer
How are you? I have been meaning **to** write **to**
you for **two** weeks now, but I have been **too**
busy at school. We have been learning all about
homophones. How are things in the forest? If
you'd like **to** catch up, meet me at **two** o'clock.
Bring your friends the squirrels, **too**.
From me!

You choose!
The boat sailed in **fair** weather.
Dad **missed** the train to work.
The boy ties a **knot** with his shoelaces.
The tired storekeeper took a **break**.
The lion had a majestic **mane**.

Silly sentences
I couldn't wait to **meet** my friends.
Because I overslept, I **missed** the bus.
I had a long **wait** for the next bus.
The mouse got his **tail** caught.

Match up!
interrupt, submerge, antibiotic, return, automatic

You choose!
I am going to **recycle** these bottles.
When Suzy kept talking, the teacher asked her to
please not **interrupt** in the middle of the lesson.
In the intermission of a show, you can buy **refreshments**.
The famous film star was asked for his **autograph**.
The crocodile was completely **submerged** under
the water.

Which one?
intercepted, interact, interlock
subtract, submarine, subject
autocracy, autopilot, automobile
reaffirm, record, reheat
antisocial, anticlimax, antidote

Cat rescue
we had, should not, did not, should not, will not, she is, she would, she is, it had, was not, she had

One-minute challenge
he's, don't, that'll, couldn't

You choose!
I've got **your** book by mistake.
They're going to the farm by bus.
Whose coat is that?
It's a really sunny day today.

Word sort

c = /k/	c = /s/	c = /sh/	c = /q/	c = /x/
carrot	cylinder	magician	cue	access
cardigan	celebrity	ocean		accident
column	mercy			except
disco	cereal			
Canada	celery			
octopus	December			

Quiz master
calf, February, Geography, vegetable, knife and scissors, island, chocolate

Letter hunt
wrinkle, san**d**wich, int**e**rest, clim**b**, lis**t**en, g**u**ide, **w**rapping, **k**neel, s**c**ience, bis**c**uit, **g**nash, disg**u**ise, fore**i**gn, cas**t**le

Word sort

/off/	/uff/	/o/	/aw/	/oo/
cough	rough	borough	ought	through
trough	enough	thorough	bought	
	tough	dough	thought	
		although		

Match the meaning
fine – A charge made for overdue items or illegally parked cars
duck – A verb meaning to move your head down quickly
wind – A strong gust of air
saw – A sharp, serrated edged cutting tool
watch – A verb meaning to look at

Match up!
goalkeeper, sunshine, bluebell, birthday, everybody or everyone, paintbrush, breakfast, anybody or anyone, backbone, fairground, halftime, upstairs

Double or not
tentacles
beetle
prickles
turtle
waddles

DK Penguin Random House

Senior Editor Deborah Lock
US Senior Editor Shannon Beatty
Editor Arpita Nath
Asst. Editor Kritika Gupta
US Educational Consultant Anne Flounders
Senior Art Editor Ann Cannings
Project Art Editor Tanvi Nathyal
Art Editors Ian Midson, Roohi Rais
Picture Researcher Sakshi Saluja
Jacket Designer Dheeraj Arora
Managing Editor Soma B. Chowdhury
Art Director Martin Wilson
DTP Designers Nand Kishor Acharya,
Ashok Kumar, Mohd. Rizwan, Dheeraj Singh
Producer, Pre-Production Dragana Puvacic
Producer Priscilla Reby

First American Edition, 2016
Published in the United States by DK Publishing
345 Hudson Street, New York, New York 10014

A catalog record for this book
is available from the Library of Congress.
ISBN 978-1-4654-5083-8

DK books are available at special discounts when purchased
in bulk for sales promotions, premiums, fund-raising, or
educational use. For details, contact: DK Publishing Special
Markets, 345 Hudson Street, New York, New York 10014
SpecialSales@dk.com

Printed and bound in China.

The publisher would like to thank the following for their kind
permission to reproduce their photographs:
(Key: a-above; b-below/bottom; c-center; f-far; l-left; r-right; t-top)
1 Dreamstime.com: Mythja (tl). **7 Dorling Kindersley:** Neil Fletcher (bl, bc). **9
Dorling Kindersley:** Cecil Williamson Collection (crb). **10 Dreamstime.com:**
Happyshoot (c). **12-13 Fotolia:** Eric Isselee (t). **12 Fotolia:** Eric Isselee (bl, bc). **19
Fotolia:** Eric Isselee (bl, bc). **20 Stockphoto.com:** thawats (cla). **24 Dreamstime.com:**
Uros Petrovic (tl). **25 Dreamstime.com:** Uros Petrovic (tr, clb). **29 Getty Images:**
Jason Edwards (cb). **32 Getty Images:** Nicole Duplaix (tl). **32-33 Corbis:** David
Watts / Visuals Unlimited. **36 Dreamstime.com:** Johannes Gerhardus Swanepoel (cr).
Fotolia: Eric Isselee (cl). **37 Dreamstime.com:** Eric Isselee (ca). **Fotolia:** Eric Isselee
(cl). **40 Fotolia:** Eric Isselee (cra). **42-43 Corbis:** Klaus Mehret / BIA / Minden
Pictures (t). **44 123RF:** Vasiliy Vishnevskiy (cla) (mole); **Dreamstime.com:** Theo
Malings (ca, br); Vchphoto (cla). **45 Dorling Kindersley:** Jerry Young (cr). **49
Fotolia:** Eric Isselee (cra). **51 Dreamstime.com:** Mythja (b). **54-55 Dreamstime.com:**
Samfoto (Background). **56 123RF.com:** Iakov Filimonov (tr). **59 Dreamstime.com:**
Marusea Turcu (tr). **62 Dorling Kindersley:** Natural History Museum, London (br).
68 Dreamstime.com: Stuartbur (bl). **68-69 Getty Images:** Tim Graham. **71 Dorling
Kindersley:** The Real Aeroplane Company (c). **Dreamstime.com:** Simone Winkler /
Eyecatchlight (cl). **iStockphoto.com:** Floortje (tc). **72-73 123RF.com:** Elena
Duvernay. **74 Dreamstime.com:** Sombra12 (ca). **75 Dreamstime.com:** Melissa King
(c). **76-77 Getty Images:** Brian J. Skerry (t). **78 Dorling Kindersley:** Jerry Young (br).
80 Dorling Kindersley: Jerry Young (tr). **Dreamstime.com:** Eric Isselee (crb). **84-85
Corbis:** Viewstock. **85 Dreamstime.com:** 350jb (ca). **86 123RF.com:** Iakov Filimonov
(tr). **90-91 naturepl.com:** Jabruson. **102-103 Dorling Kindersley:** Odds Farm Park,
High Wycombe, Bucks. **103 123RF.com:** damianpalus (c). **108 Dreamstime.com:**
Tropper2000 (cra). **110 Dorling Kindersley:** Liberty's Owl, Raptor and Reptile
Centre, Hampshire, UK (bl). **112 123RF.com:** Isabelle Kõhn (cl); Konstantin
Kalishko (cr). **Alamy Images:** Brian Hagiwara (tr). **114-115 123RF.com:** Eric Isselee.
114 123RF.com: Eric Isselee (bl). **115 Stockphoto.com:** GlobalP (bl). **116 Corbis:**
Eric and David Hosking (br). **Dreamstime.com:** Musat Christian (cr). **Fotolia:**
uwimages (cl). **117 123RF.com:** Eric Isselee (cla, cb); Kati Molin (ca). **Dorling
Kindersley:** British Wildlife Centre, Surrey, UK (bl).**Dreamstime.com:** Sombra12 (br).
iStockphoto.com: DreamyHarry (cra). **122 Dreamstime.com:** Isselee (tl). **123 123RF.
com:** Kseniya Abramova (cla). **124 Fotolia:** Eric Isselee (br). **125 Fotolia:** Eric Isselee
(tr, cl). **126 Dorling Kindersley:** Jerry Young (br). **Dreamstime.com:** Sombra12 (cr).
127 123RF.com: Konstantin Kalishko (br)
Jacket images: **Front: Dreamstime.com:** Milos Tasic (tl)

All images © Dorling Kindersley Limited
For further information see: www.dkimages.com

A WORLD OF IDEAS:
SEE ALL THERE IS TO KNOW
www.dk.com

Note to parents

Spelling in English is not that easy. There are many rules and many exceptions to the rules, and also some words that follow no rule at all! Children need to be encouraged to try out spelling and gain confidence to spell independently. They need to build up skills so that they are not reliant on adults or dictionaries to make a good attempt at spelling an unfamiliar word.

Reading is a great help with spelling and it actually does not matter what they are reading. Your child could love comics, or sports magazines, fiction or non-fiction; it is the quantity and reading for pleasure that makes the difference. Reading a lot exposes children to the spellings, so they start to recognize when they have spelled something wrong because it does not look right on the page.

Children should also start by using phonics and what they know about spelling for their first attempt. If a very young child uses what they know about phonics to spell a word, they are starting well and using the correct skills. Older children start to recognize some of the other spelling conventions, too.

This book teaches the spelling rules, where they exist, but also looks at how children learn spellings, encouraging them to find the ways that suit them best. Trying out spelling is a good way of seeing if it looks right and should be encouraged as an important part of the learning process.

It is also important to consider spelling as a tool, not an end goal. Spelling is useful because it enables us to become better writers. If we learn how to spell a great word and use it in writing, this is more important than being able to spell a great many words but not use the words when we write. If you see spelling as part of the writing process, you will be helping your child to become a better writer, not just a better speller.